SIMPLY
SUSTAINABLE

Simply SUSTAINABLE

Simple Behaviors for Sustainable Living

SHILA WATTAMWAR

Library of Congress Control Number: 2024909479

ISBN: 978-1-954676-94-7 (paperback)   978-1-954676-93-0 (hardback)   978-1-954676-95-4 (ebook)

Although this publication is designed to provide accurate information about the subject matter, the publisher and the author assume no responsibility for any errors, inaccuracies, omissions, or inconsistencies herein. This publication is intended as a resource, however, it is not intended as a replacement for direct and personalized professional services.

Editors: Deborah Froese, Christian Pacheco

Cover and Interior Design: Emma Elzinga

Printed in the United States of America

First Edition

Indigo River Publishing

3 West Garden Street, Ste. 718

Pensacola, FL 32502

www.indigoriverpublishing.com

Ordering Information:

Quantity sales: Special discounts are available on quantity purchases by corporations, associations, and others. For details, contact the publisher at the address above.

Orders by US trade bookstores and wholesalers: Please contact the publisher at the address above.

With Indigo River Publishing, you can always expect great books, strong voices, and meaningful messages. Most importantly, you'll always find . . . words worth reading.

> *"If we choose to live a more sustainable lifestyle now, our actions will shape how our children treat the world."*
>
> **— SHILA WATTAMWAR**

Holistic SUSTAINABLY

Simply Sustainable: Simple Behaviors for Sustainable Living provides two basic tools for implementing a viable, cleaner lifestyle: information and action. Geared toward people of all ages, this book will help you and your family understand the environmental and social challenges facing us now, and at the same time, discover actionable choices that you can neatly incorporate into your everyday lives for more sustainable, healthier living.

In a world where we are often encouraged to use more sustainable practices (recycling, composting, water conservation, and so on), without understanding why these behaviors are important, it is easy for people to become overwhelmed by the concept of sustainability. Often, we indulge various practices that seem trendy, but without the education and connection necessary to form new habits. Just as we are far more likely to take vitamins or go for that jog if we understand the benefits, we are far more likely to commit to sustainability if we understand the negative ramifications of doing otherwise.

SUSTAINABILITY *Wheels*

DECREASING ATMOSPHERIC GREEN HOUSE GAS EMISSIONS

CARBON AVOIDANCE

CARBON REMOVAL

CARBON CAPTURE & STORAGE

- Afforestation
- Reforestation
- Soil Restoration
- Avoid Deforestation
- Preserve Carbon Sinks
- Less Consumption
- Renewable Energy
- Avoid Excess Emissions
- Wate Managment *(Reduce, Reuse, Recycle)*
- Use Biodegradable Raw Materials

SOCIAL EQUALITY AND DIVERSITY (GENER, RACE, AND ECONOMIC)

RACIAL, GENDER, AND ECONOMIC EQUALITY AND DIVERSITY

- Fair Access to Clean Water
- Respect for all Populations
- Fair Wages
- Fair Representation
- Fair Benefits
- Safe Working Environment
- Fair Access to Education
- Fair Access to Healthcare
- Fair Access to Food
- Fair Access to Shelter

Simply Sustainable: Simple Behaviors for Sustainable Living looks at change realistically. By making good choices now—and making those choices habitual—you can implement a positive, systemic influence over the environment and social climates for generations to come.

Within these pages, we look at five areas to promote holistic sustainability: **food, drink, fashion, home**, and **investments**. You'll find one educational fact about sustainability per week along with a choice you can make to address that fact. Just think! Over the course of one year, you can learn 52 facts and integrate 52 related sustainable choices into your life.

Sustainable **EATING**	*Sustainable* **DRINKING**	*Sustainable* **FASHION**	*Sustainable* **HOME**	*Sustainable* **INVESTING**

May you find these sustainable behaviors both achievable and compelling.

THANK YOU,
Shila Wattamwar

Fact

It takes 2,720 liters of water to make one t-shirt. *That's how much an average person drinks over three years!* [1]

Action

Donate old clothes instead of throwing them away so they can be further used.

Fact

As of March 2023, over 7,000 mutual funds that considered sustainability factors in their investment thesis were available worldwide, with approximately $2.5 trillion invested in them.[2]

Action

Learn about the wide array of sustainable exchange-traded funds (ETFs) and mutual funds available to you. You can find this information online, on your brokerage platform, at your bank, or through a financial advisor.

"**Sustainable investing is personal investing.** It allows us the opportunity to invest in a way that aligns with our values. You can find sustainable investing choices that are broad and others that are more focused on specific areas such as climate change, ex-tobacco, gender equality, and more.

– SHILA WATTAMWAR

"The best way to find yourself
is to lose yourself
in the service of others."

– MAHATMA GANDHI

Fact

Median household income in 2020 was roughly $46,000 for African Americans and $55,000 for Hispanics compared to $75,000 and $95,000 for white and Asian households respectively.[3]

Action

Volunteer to help support the needs of an underserved community. Community organizations or the education system are great places to look for opportunities to build better lives.

Fact

The US produces nearly 117 million metric tons of greenhouse gas emissions annually from air conditioning. This is equivalent to the carbon dioxide emissions of 24.5 million passenger vehicles.[4]

Action

Use natural methods of temperature control when possible. For example, use fans and sweaters instead of turning up air conditioners or heaters.

"There's a trick to composting that you may not realize when you first begin—make sure you store the food scraps in your freezer to avoid any fruit flies. Also, for those in NYC, download the NYC Composting app to see where your nearby free composting bin is and always make sure to check if it's full before making the trip!"

— MILENA STOJCESKA

Fact

Composting has significant benefits for our world by:

✳ Significantly cutting down on the amount of trash in a landfill.

✳ Enriching the soil with nutrients from compost, which reduces the need for chemical fertilizers and pesticides.

✳ Increasing the soil's ability to retain moisture, thus reducing soil runoff and helping to prevent erosion.

✳ Sequestering carbon which means helping to remove it from the atmosphere.[5]

Action

Consider how much you can compost in your home and research local composting options.

Fact

If all computers in the US were Energy Star compliant, approximately $1.8 billion dollars in energy costs could be saved each year. This would in return lead to a decrease in greenhouse gas emission equivalent to that of two million cars.[6]

Action

When purchasing your next computer, learn more about Energy Star compliant computer options. Start by checking out www.EnergyStar.gov. You may even find energy rebates that will save you even more money!

"At one point, I became acutely aware of how many paper towels we were using everyday, and I started feeling badly about the amount of waste we were creating. **So, I made a simple switch to reusable Swedish dishcloths. They are just as effective. This change has dramatically cut down the amount of paper towels we use and saved us money.** The dishcloths can be quickly rinsed and reused, and they also dry reasonable fast. It makes it tenable to reuse them multiple times throughout the day. And they can be thrown in with the regular laundry every few days."

— LAVANYA VENKATESWARAN

Fact

By 2050, due to rapid population growth and urbanization, annual **waste generation is expected to increase by 73 percent** percent from 2020 levels. This would mean 3.88 billion metric tonnes of waste in 2050.[7]

Action

Reduce your waste by purchasing a reusable water bottle or coffee cup instead of disposable ones.

Fact

Growing mushrooms requires less water than many other fruits and vegetables. It also uses land very effectively. One square foot of land can produce 7.1 pounds of mushrooms per year with far less carbon emissions than many other type of vegetables. In addition, mushrooms are a great source of compost. They strengthen soil structure by more effectively breaking down key nutrients and can even grow using agricultural waste such as corn husks, saw dust, banana leaves, and so on.[8]

Action

Order a new innovative mushroom dish from your favorite restaurant or try making one at home. The wide variety of mushrooms available can cater to several different taste preferences.

"*Mushrooms to me are great teachers, imparting knowledge through the change they create in their environment.*"

— BARIS SONMEZ, Founder, LifeCap Farms

Fact

Not only do most single-use cotton pads require unsustainable amounts of water to manufacture, but the plastic also often mixed with the cotton means these pads are not biodegradable or recyclable.[9]

Action

Use reusable makeup wipes to reduce waste.

Fact

One full-grown tree will absorb as much as 48 pounds of carbon pollution every year.[10]

Action

Work with an organization to plant a tree at least once a year. Local arboretums and nature reserves often provide people with opportunities to do so.

"For any tree planted in a community, there are immensely priceless short and long term social, economic and physical benefits that live with the community forever. Trees yield water recharge, the attraction of butterflies and pollinators, fertile soils for healthier food production, medicine... and biodiversity opportunities that enhance dignified livelihoods for communities. Tree planting reunites people with the natural environment and makes apparent the basic links between climate systems, our physical world, and our communities."

— TABI JODA and KAI CASH

Fact

Almost **half of the wine industry's carbon footprint comes from shipping and distribution** since most wine is packaged in bottles that are heavier than the wine itself.[11]

Action

Look for wine producers that utilize bulk shipping methods that involve transporting wine in huge tanks and then bottled in the country of sale. By reducing weight, the carbon footprint (and cost) of shipping is reduced.

Fact

Twenty-two billion pairs of shoes are thrown away every year, and each of them can take 30 to 40 years to decompose in a landfill.[12]

Action

Drop off old sneakers to textile recycling bins in your area (often located near shopping malls). Textile recycling companies can upcycle old sneaker materials into products such as insulation, surfacing for playgrounds and courts, and carpet padding.

> "*I bought a pair of running shoes from the Re-Vivo resell site where they sell professionally refurbished Vivo shoes and they came to me in really fantastic condition, **in fact they looked pretty much new to me.**"*
>
> — **CAL MAJOR**, Ambassador, Vivofarefoot

"Embracing sustainability is a dual commitment—to the planet and my well-being. By choosing local, I cut emissions, support my community, and savor healthier meals. It's more than a responsibility; it's a delightful journey of conscious living that nourishes both me and the Earth."

— AYSU SECKIN

Fact

Sourcing fresh food from local farms:

❋ Helps boost the local economy.
❋ Reduces the need for shipping and thus lowers the carbon footprint.
❋ Encourages innovative sustainable farming techniques.
❋ Provides fresh and delicious tasting food.

Action

Go to a restaurant that locally sources most of their ingredients. Restaurants that do this typically highlight the fact on their websites or on their menus.

Fact

According to the World Bank, **businesses and individuals pay more than $1 trillion in bribes every year.**[13]

Action

Consider looking into **Socially Responsible Investing** (SRI) which screens funds for negative and positive impacts on society and local communities. You can find great free resources online such as screeners on https://www.morningstar.com and https://eft.com/tools.

27

"Whatever affects one directly,
affects all indirectly."

– MARTIN LUTHER KING, JR.

Fact

According to the FBI, *there are typically around 6,000 hate crimes every year.* About 60 percent of them racially motivated or related to ethnicity/national origin bias.[14]

Action

Learn about and/or experience a different culture. The more we understand other cultural perspectives, the more we can appreciate our differences and support each other, resulting in a more equitable society.

Fact

Worldwide, **785 million people live without clean drinking water.**[15]

Action

Appreciate the clean water you have by not wasting the water you can access. Examples of water conservation include turning off faucets while brushing your teeth, taking shorter showers, checking for water leaks, and buying water efficient appliances where possible.

"I'm focused on learning how to **take waste outputs and turn them into economic inputs** for myself and/or others. This is show we can make our economy truly sustainable."

— GRACEY, Circular Economy Advocate

Fact

According to the Global Plastic Action Partnership, World Economic Forum, and other studies, scientists expect **there could be more plastic than fish in the ocean by 2050.**[16]

Action

Choose reusable items for your travel utensils, cloth bags, and food storage containers instead of single-use plastic alternatives.

Fact

Approximately **one-third of the food produced for human consumption every year is wasted or lost.** This is equivalent to about 1.32 billion metric tons and valued at one trillion USD—and enough to feed three billion people.[17]

Action

Consider the different ways you can upcycle food waste at home:

❋ Soak banana peels overnight and use that water to water your plants.

❋ Blend wilted greens and freeze them into ice cubes for smoothies instead of throwing them away.

❋ Make your own facial masks with leftover fruits and vegetables.

"I look at everything through a longevity lens. To me, sustainability means asking, 'have I used to this to the fullest and how else can it be used?'"

— ASMERET BERHE-LUMAX,
OneLoveCommunityFridge.org

Fact

The coffee we enjoy depends on **25 million coffee producers, 10 million hectares of coffee farms,** and the continued ability to sustain these people and resources.[18]

Action

Purchase coffee that has one of the following labels to indicate fair wages and minimized environmental effects:

✳ **FAIR-TRADE:** Ensures fair working environment.

✳ **RAINFOREST** Alliance Certified: Focuses on preserving the biodiversity of the coffee plantation, as well as banning the use of harmful chemicals and ensuring fair wages.

✳ **ORGANIC:** Bans the use of synthetic pesticides, herbicides and fertilizers; also requires farmers to use methods that prevent soil erosion.

Fact

The footprint of one hamburger is approximately 650 gallons of water. Compare that to the footprint of one bowl of lentils at 57 gallons of water or one bowl of salad at about 21 gallons of water.[19]

Action

Eat at least three vegan meals per week. You can find many delicious recipes on websites such as So Vegan, The Chutney Life, and Plant You.[20]

"When I make it a point to eat mostly plant-based meals over the course of a week or a few weeks, I find that I'm more energetic throughout the day and less likely to go for that second cup of coffee."

— ANOOP WATTAMWAR, MD

"*Encouraging people to make conscious choices when it comes to fashion* and *purchasing fast fashion is very important.*"

– **ANI DIMITROV**, Ani's Boutique

Fact

It takes one kilogram of cotton to produce a pair of jeans, and that cotton uses 7,500 to 10,000 liters of water. **This is equivalent to what an average person drinks over 10 years.**[21]

Action

Be careful to buy only the clothing you need and avoid the impulse to make purchases based on pressures such as social media advertising.

Fact

The travel and tourism industry accounts for roughly 8 percent of the world's carbon emissions.[22]

Action

The next time you travel for a vacation, **choose a hotel that employs sustainable practices.** Some examples of those sustainable practices include minimizing daily laundry, reducing dependency on single use plastic (water bottles, utensils, and so on), investing in renewable energy methods, harvesting rain-water, and utilizing eco-friendly soaps, shampoos, and cleaning products. Hotels will often highlight their sustainable practices on their website, so check them out before you book your room.

"By changing small things in your travel behavior you can make a difference. And if you do this with millions of travelers, you can make a big impact on the environment and local tourism all over the world."

— MAARTEN DE RUITER, CEO WeTravelEco.

"As a cardiologist, I am using more remote monitoring techniques for pacemaker evaluations and heart monitors. This reduces travel for patients and the environmental factors associated with office visits and hospitals. This is especially helpful in rural areas where patients travel for hours to see a cardiologist."

— SHEILA NADIMINTI, Cardiologist

Fact

In 2021, *passenger cars accounted for 58 percent of the fuels emitted by the transportation sector* in the US (approximately 17 percent of all total fossil fuels in the US).[23]

Action

Whenever possible, walk, bike, or take public transportation to get to your destination. If a single person switches a 20-mile commute by car to a bus or train ride, they can reduce their annual CO_2 emissions by 20 pounds per day. That's equal to a ten percent reduction in all greenhouse gases produced by a typical two-adult, two-car household.[24]

Fact

Most conventional and popular **household cleaning products have a significant negative carbon emissions and water waste impact** through heavy manufacturing processes and packaging.[25]

Action

Make a DIY non-toxic cleaning solution. Chemicals such as bleach, air fresheners, and wood polish, and cleaners for everything from ovens to carpets and glass can easily be made at home with just a few common ingredients like lemon and vinegar. Or try shopping for sustainable house cleaners that minimize the use of water and use plastic alternatives in their packaging.

"90 percent of a liquid facial cleanser is just water which is typically stored in single-use packaging (most of which is never recycled). Our skincare at Seadrop consciously designs formulations to eliminate single-use waste and can use biodegradable packaging, eliminating the need for single-use plastics altogether."

– SERENA ADVANI,
Founder & CEO of Seadrop Skincare

Fact

Ingredients used in cosmetics such as palm oil, petroleum, and wood-based ingredients are major contributors to deforestation around the world. *They're found in 70 percent of our cosmetics.*[26]

Action

Choose cosmetics that come from a sustainable brand and use more sustainable and organic ingredients and non-plastic or recycled packaging. Seadrop Skin Care creates water-less skincare tablets in order to reduce water waste.[27] SixGldn creates skin care that focuses on the waste and plastic reduction in its packaging.[28]

Fact

In 2021, Over $500 billion flowed into mutual funds that considered a company's environmental, social and governance risks. These investments contributed to a 55 percent growth in assets under management (AUM) in ESG-integrated products.[29]

Action

Read an article about sustainable investing so that you can understand what it means in more detail and make prudent investment decisions that align with your values.

"Despite a slowdown in 2023 due to market headwinds and regulatory uncertainty, *the demand from investors for sustainable investing remains resilient,* and advisors are responding to that demand. Approximately one third [or more than 29,000] advisors using the Envestnet platform are using sustainable investment funds on behalf of their clients, representing over $35B in assets*."

– KILEY MILLER,
Portfolio Manager

Data as of June 30, 2023

51

"Watching people learn about food through the lens of sustainability and the health of our planet is the most impactful work I have ever been a part of. **Food is medicine for both people and the planet** and is the key to healthier communities and a healthier earth. Bringing people back to the basics of food and showing them how simple it can be to make a difference is what I love most."

— THEODORA FONTAS,
Chefs4Impact

Fact

Three billion metric tons of CO2-equivalent chemicals were produced *by transporting food for human consumption each year*.[30]

Action

Plant a vegetable or herb garden in your backyard, consider purchasing a small portable hydroponic device to grow salad vegetables and herbs inside your house, or buy seasonal, locally grown vegetables. By minimizing the food supply chain, you reduce the carbon footprint of bringing food to your kitchen.

Fact

Plastic straws are neither biodegradable nor recyclable. For this reason, they contribute a significant amount of pollution especially affecting our marine life. It is estimated that over eight billion plastic straws pollute the world's beaches.[31]

Action

Use a metal or bamboo straw instead of a single use plastic straw. They are now available at most major retail stores.

"As a mother, leaving my two little boys [and potentially their little ones] with a healthy planet is my primary motivator to live more sustainably. What also motivates me is learning over the years that a little can go a long way if we all do our part. Making sure we compost, maximize recycling of all household items and clothes, and even cut paper towel pieces in half, are a few of the small things we've been doing for some time. I'm excited to learn more simple acts that we can take with our kids!"

— RADHIKA LAKHANI,
Founder of Consciousness with Rad

Fact

Over the next decade, *the number of green jobs in the U.S. is expected to grow by another 114,000, or 9 percent.*[32]

Action

Talk to your kids about sustainability and the options and benefits associated with them. This will help them better prepare for creating the sustainable world of the future.

Fact

Of the world's 75 million factory workers, **only 2 percent are paid fairly**.[33]

Action

Read about the factory practices of your favorite large brands, especially in apparel or footwear. *How fairly do they pay? How many hours must an employee work and what kind of environment do they work in?* This investigation may take time, but if we are interested in supporting people and the planet, educating ourselves about the practices of companies we buy from may be eye-opening. It may influence future purchases.

> *"Paying good wages is not charity at all—
> it is the best kind of business."*
>
> **– HENRY FORD**

Fact

The plastic cling wrap so frequently found in our kitchens **is not recyclable or compostable.**[34]

Action

Purchase a multi-use product such as cloth or beeswax wrap.

Fact

Phantom loads occur when devices such as toasters, coffee makers and phone chargers continue to draw electricity even while they are turned off. Simple acts such as unplugging some of these devices when not in use, can save nearly **80 million tons of carbon dioxide,** the equivalent of the annual carbon emissions from about **15 million cars a year** across the US.[35]

Action

Put a family member in charge of unplugging small electronic appliances when not being used. This is a great way to get older kids involved and teach them the importance of using energy wisely.

Fact

The world has lost over two-thirds of its wildlife in 50 years.[36]

Action

Tropical forests, which host significant numbers of wildlife, are rapidly being cut down for palm oil procurement. Before you do your shopping this week, check out the companies you typically buy from. *Purchase products from companies committed to using sustainably produced palm oil or alternatives to palm oil in their products.* These commitments can usually be found on company websites.

Fact

Producing one glass of milk generates about double the emissions created by the production of plant-based alternative milks and uses two to three times the amount of water.[37]

Action

Use a plant-based milk for your coffee and foods like smoothies. Oatly oak milk is one of my personal favorites.[38]

"The most difficult part of being vegan is waking up at 5:00 a.m. to milk the almonds."

— ANONYMOUS

Fact

By 2050, there will be about 2 billion more mouths to feed than there were in 2023. To meet this need, *the worldwide water demand will increase by 55%*.[39]

Action

Watch a sustainability documentary and learn more about the state of water on our planet. With a quick internet search, you'll find there are many to choose from. Some popular titles include Conspiracy: *The Sustainability Secret; Minimalist; Kiss the Ground: How the Food You Eat Can Reverse Climate Change, Heal Your Body & Ultimately Save Our World;* and *Wasted! The story of Food Waste*.[40]

Fact

Doubling the useful life of clothing from one year to two years **reduces emissions by 24 percent.**[41]

Action

Find a fun second-hand or consignment store in your area, or **plan a clothing swap party with some friends.**

> "'Second-hand' should not be looked down on; in fact, it's the opposite. The fact that something can have a 'second life' means it's high quality made. And we should all strive for quality over quantity."
>
> — EMILY SCHWARTZ,
> Founder & CEO, The Resale Stylist

Fact

In 2022, the natural resources required to sustain one human on our planet were estimated to be 1.5 global hectares. However, humanity's ecological footprint—the amount of resources we are actually demanding from the earth per person—is 2.7 global hectares, or almost twice what we actually need. The gap between what we need and what we use is concerning. **We do not currently have enough resources to handle the load of our consumption needs.**[42]

Action

It is important to learn about the impacts of our consumption. **Subscribe to a sustainability podcast** to learn more about the impacts we're causing. Two very interesting podcast series are Brown Girl Green and How to Save the Planet. Both are available on Apple Podcasts and Spotify.[43]

Fact

Sustainable fashion habits mean more than simply purchasing your clothing from sustainable fashion brands. Those brands may **minimize their impact on the environment** through production practices and biodegradability, but they still contribute to the 92 million tonnes of textile waste globally every year.[44]

Action

The most effective way of engaging sustainable fashion is to *purchase fewer clothes and wear the ones you already own for longer.*

"**Sustainability is quality.** The more you make garments out of materials that last, the more you're able to reduce consumption. So buy better and buy less"

— MONICA BOTKIER & OLGA KAPUSTINA,
ChosenWoven

Fact

A solid bar shampoo leaves a significantly lower water footprint compared to its liquid counterparts due to lower water consumption—and not only in the way we use it. Manufacturing and packaging use less water too. In general, the water footprint of a solid bar shampoo is approximately 575 liters less than a bottle of liquid shampoo.[45]

Action

Use a solid bar shampoo at least once a week.

Fact

As seafood is a significant source of animal protein for over three billion people globally, **the seafood industry is increasingly becoming exploited and overfished.** For example, the sea urchin in Sicilian waters is at risk for extinction.[46] Also, the Atlantic Ocean is almost 60% overfished.[47] This is leading to significant issues related to marine biodiversity, increase in pollution and deterioration of coastal communities.

Action

Purchasing seafood with one of the following sustainability labels, Marine Stewardship Council (MSC), the Aquaculture Stewardship Council (ASC), the Monterey Bay Aquarium's Seafood Watch, indicates that the fisheries or fish farms are committed to responsible practices to protect and optimize marine ecosystems.

"*Much of wild-caught fish goes through processors, distributors, wholesalers, and retailers until it finally reaches the consumer. We deserve fresher seafood, fewer people handling the product.*"

– KYLE LEE,

CEO and Founder of Alaskan Salmon Co.

"By working on my podcast, *Sustainability with Soren*, I have gotten to know lots of cool and very interesting solutions that help with sustainability. For example, **people are inventing new ways to capture the methane gas that comes out of cows.** *Even the NBA is working on sustainability!*"

— SOREN WATTAMWAR,
Kid contributor, SustainableMe.Today

Fact

So many **interesting innovations help drive a more sustainable economy** by effectively using natural materials. Some examples include using the mycelium mushroom plant for plant-based leathers, sugar-cane leaves for compostable dishware, and nut shells for non-plastic planters.

Action

Take time this week to explore some of these new innovations with your kids. Get your kids to choose the innovations that excite them the most and show your support with your purchasing power.

Fact

Modern dishwashers use less water and less energy to heat that water, creating a smaller carbon footprint than washing dishes by hand.[48]

Action

When it comes to washing the dishes, *go ahead and load the dishwasher.*

Fact

The period between Thanksgiving and New Year's Day sees an extra million tons of waste generated per week.[49]

Action

Reduce consumption and waste by gifting an experience—such as a no-site or virtual cooking class—rather than a product. Consider saving your gift bags to reuse next year.

Fact

Energy-efficient light bulbs use almost 75 percent less energy than incandescent light bulbs.[50]

Action

For the most frequently used lights in your home, **switch from incandescent light bulbs to energy-efficient light bulbs.**

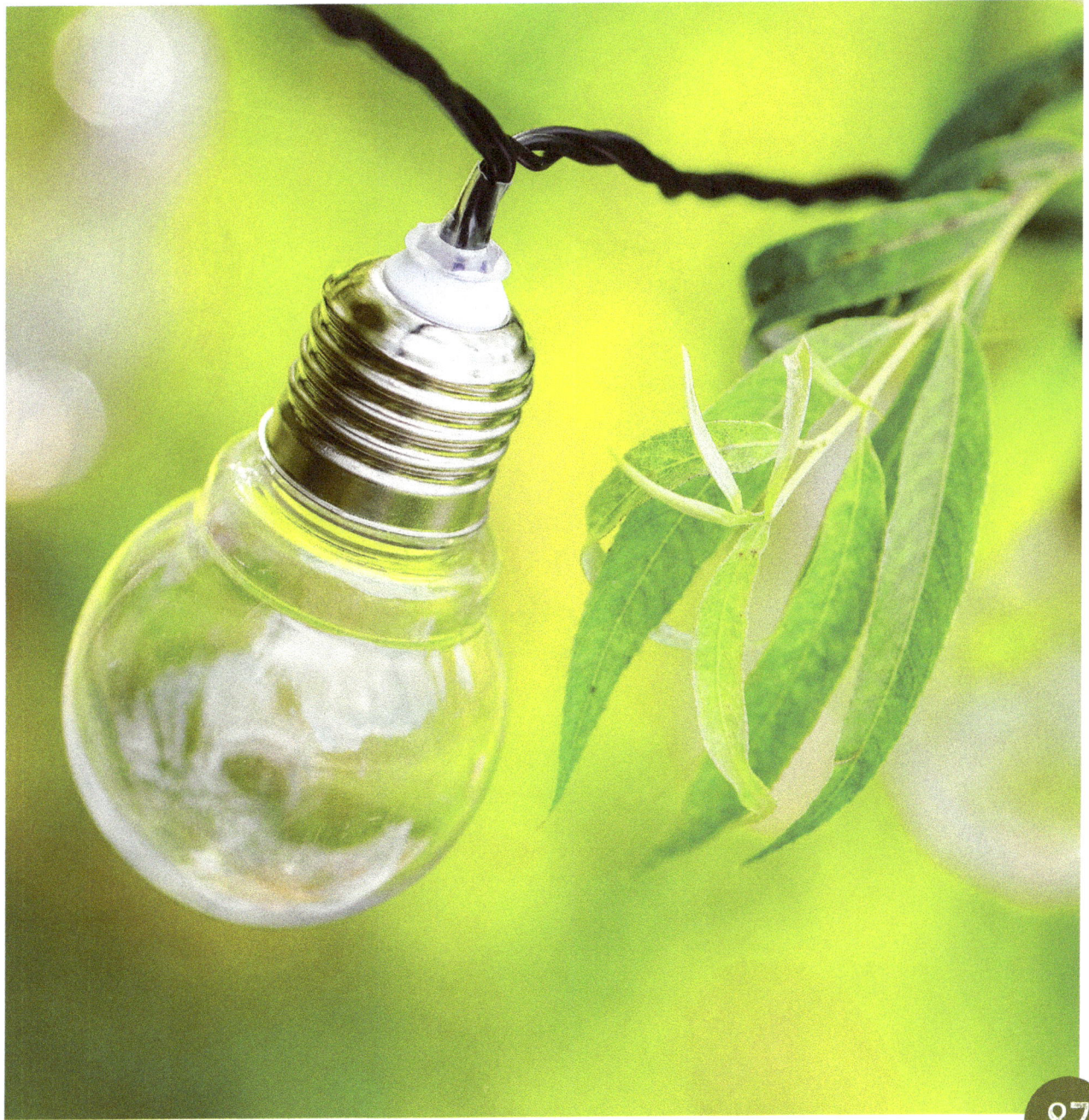

"Nature is such a wonderful thing. Its so beautiful and you can spend hours just wandering in it. Instead of going on a device, spend a few hours hiking, bike riding or walking. Or try a scavenger hunt! Reconnecting with nature will also help clear your mind and make an impact physically and mentally."

— KARINA GUPTA,

Kid contributor, SustainableMe.Today

Fact

One tree will soak up to 2,300 gallons of storm water runoff annually. *That's equivalent to the water you'll drink in 12 years.*[51]

Action

Go for a walk outdoors and explore the natural environment around you. Spending time in nature increases awareness of human impact and helps you feel a greater sense of responsibility for sustaining and preserving it.

Fact

Sustainable wineries employ techniques that minimize waste and environmental damage such as water conservation and waste composting. Sustainable vineyards may use birds of prey to eat troublesome insects or create insectaries (areas of plants that attract bugs) instead of using harmful pesticides. Sustainable wines are certified through party verification of these practices.[52]

Action

Next time you buy a bottle of wine, **look for an official sustainable certification on the label of the wine.**

Fact

Flights account for approximately 50 percent of the carbon footprint of tourism.[53]

Action

Take one trip a year that uses a more sustainable mode of travel; for example, train or ferry.

Fact

Fifty percent of the plastics produced every year are for single use. This equal 380 million tons of plastic.[54]

Action

Try to reuse plastic items. For example, wash zipper bags as often as possible.

"I reuse the zipper bag that I take to school for a snack for 5 days. Every day, I quickly rinse it out if its dirty, and its ready for me the next morning. Its pretty easy, and I think everyone should try it."

— AVIN WATTAMWAR,
Kid Contributor, SustainbleMe.Today

"In 2017, we installed solar panels on our home. The initiative to install panels was not only related to sustainability but also to a financial investment. Solar panels allowed us to get renewable energy for our home, reduce our electric bills, and also receive monthly SREC credits. In five years we were able to recover our investment on the panels and enjoy a sustainable source of electricity for our home."

— SHREYA MADDIWAR

Fact

Solar panels help significantly reduce carbon dioxide emissions. They emit 24.2 grams of CO2 per kWh over their lifetime compared to natural gas energy production which emits 470 g of CO2/kWh, and coal production which emits 979 g of CO2/kWh.[55]

Action

Many states offer tax incentives or subsidies for the installation of solar panels. Investigate what supports might be available to help you install solar panels in your home.

Fact

An increasing number of sustainability initiatives are appearing on shareholder proxy ballots. Some of these include increased disclosure on workflow diversity statistics and climate change management initiatives. For example, Amazon's vote bulletin looked at disclosing more information on the company's approach to reducing plastic waste arising from their products and services.[56]

Action

As an investor, make sure to vote your eligible proxies for any shares you hold directly.

"My family and I try our best to make small changes in our home to help our planet. A common quote used in our home is "Be the Change." One of the changes we have made is to eliminate paper napkins and paper towel usage in our home. We have used only cloth napkins and reusable towels for the past three years."

— JAYMEE NAIK

Fact

Disposable paper products such as cleaning wipes and paper towels *account for 13 billion pounds of waste annually.*[57]

Action

Use reusable cloth napkins instead of disposable paper napkins.

Fact

A temperature rise of two degrees will lead to,

* 18 percent biodiversity loss.
* $80 billion in damage to crops.
* 30 percent more populations exposed to flooding.[58]

Action

Tell at least one other person about a sustainable action or choice you've made recently and encourage them to do the same. By bringing more people on board for sustainable choices globally, we can help avoid the harsh reality of climate change.

Sustainable

About the AUTHOR

Shila began her sustainability journey over ten years ago in the sustainable investing space where she sat on the executive team for one of the largest ESG rating firms globally.

Through that experience, Shila learned that engaging three key stakeholders—investors, companies and people—is essential. They are equally important.

✳ Investors can help drive capital to companies that are addressing important sustainability issues.

✳ Companies have the power to meaningfully bring sustainable solutions to people at scale.

✳ People need to be empowered through knowledge to demand provision of those sustainable solutions.

With this understanding, she started her platform, SustainableMe! which encourages people to bring sustainability into the everyday contexts of their lives for a more holistic lifestyle.

Shila sits on the executive leadership team at RE Tech Advisors, an advisory firm dedicated to furthering the sustainability activities of real estate assets, and is also the founder of Radiant Global Advisory, an independent advisory service that helps companies find sustainability solutions to grow their businesses while amplifying their impacts.

Shila sits on the Fast Company Impact Council, an invitation-only collective of innovative leaders, and she is the co-chair of the board for Chefs4Impact, a non-profit organization focused on food sustainability.

Shila hopes to amplify her own impact through the work she does, as well as through her wonderful family, where her 12-yr-old son, Soren, has already joined her mission through his podcast, Sustainability with Soren, available on Spotify.

Endnotes

1   Julie Malone, "It Takes 2,700 Liters of Water to Make a T-Shirt," Triple Pundit, February 6, 2013, https://www.triplepundit.com/story/2013/it-takes-2700-liters-water-make-t-shirt/54321.

2   Institute for Sustainable Finance, "Despite Market Challenges, Demand for Sustainable Funds Remains Strong," Morgan Stanley, February 15, 2023, https://www.morganstanley.com/ideas/sustainable-funds-performance-demand.

3   Janice Bowdler and Benjamin Harris, "Racial Inequality in the United States," U.S. Department of Treasury, July 21, 2022, https://home.treasury.gov/news/featured-stories/racial-inequality-in-the-united-states.

4   Office of Energy Saver, "Air Conditioning," U.S. Department of Energy, Home Comfort, accessed January 19, 2024, https://www.energy.gov/energysaver/air-conditioning.

5   United States Environmental Protection Agency, "Benefits of Using your Finished Compost," EPA, December 18, 2023, https://www.epa.gov/recycle/composting-home#benefits

6   Paul Kirvan, "Pros and cons of Energy Star," Tech Target, April 2023, https://www.techtarget.com/searchdatacenter/definition/Energy-Star#:~:text=The%20EPA%20estimated%20that%2C%20if%20every%20U.S.%20household,more%20than%20those%20produced%20by%202.7%20million%20cars.

7   The World Bank, "Solid Waste Management," The World Bank, February 11, 2022, https://www.worldbank.org/en/topic/urbandevelopment/brief/solid-waste-management.

8   Lizzy Rosenberg, "Mushrooms are Considered to be the Most Sustainable Vegetable — Here's Why," American Mushroom Institute, January 21, 2021, https://www.americanmushroom.org/news/2021/01/01/ami/mushrooms-are-considered-to-be-the-most-sustainable-vegetable-here-s-why/.

Diana Cox, "The Ultimate Guide to Mushroom Compost: Benefits, Uses, and How to Make it?" The Gardening Talk, February 23, 2023, https://thegardeningtalk.com/the-ultimate-guide-to-mushroom-compost-benefits-uses-and-how-to-make-it/.

9   Manisha Taggar, "Reusable cotton pads," Holland & Barrett, March 21, 2022, https://www.hollandandbarrett.com/the-health-hub/natural-beauty/clean-beauty/clean-beauty-skincare/reusable-cotton-pads/efits & Top Picks | Holland & Barrett (hollandandbarrett.com)

10   Joanna Stancil "The Power of One Tree - The Very Air We Breathe," U.S. Department of Agriculture, March 17, 2015, https://www.usda.gov/media/blog/2015/03/17/power-one-tree-very-air-we-breathe.

11   Natalya Guseva, "What can the wine industry teach us about sustainability?" World Economic Forum, July 27, 2021, https://www.weforum.org/agenda/2021/07/what-can-the-wine-industry-teach-us-about-sustainability/.

12   Peter Dennis, "Shoe waste: how consumption became culture," Circular, September 13, 2022, https://www.circularonline.co.uk/features/circular-trainers-how-consumption-became-culture/#:~:text=Given%20the%20vast%20market%20across%20the%20globe%2C%20it%E2%80%99s,30-40%20years%20for%20just%20one%20pair%20to%20decompose.

13   Carlos Ferreyra and Till Hartmann, "What are the costs of corruption?" World Bank Blogs, December 22, 2022, https://blogs.worldbank.org/governance/what-are-costs-corruption.

14   Community Relations Service, "FBI Releases Supplement to the 2021 Hate Crime Statistics," U.S. Department of Justice, April 4, 2003, https://www.justice.gov/crs/highlights/2021-hate-crime-statistics.

15   "Drinking-water," World Health Organization, September 13, 2023, https://www.who.int/news-room/fact-sheets/detail/drinking-water.

16   Mario Ritter, "Oceans To Hold More Plastic Than Fish by 2050," February 28, 2016, VOA News, https://learningenglish.voanews.com/a/oceans-could-hold-more-plastics-than-fish-2050/3166848.html.

17   World Food Programme, "5 facts about food waste and hunger," World Food Program, June 2, 2020, https://www.wfp.org/stories/5-facts-about-food-waste-and-hunger.

18   "People Need Coffee to Thrive," Sustainable Coffee Challenge, January 25, 2024, https://www.sustaincoffee.org/about/.

19   "What is the Water Footprint of...?" Water Footprint Calculator, July 15, 2022, https://www.watercalculator.org/footprint/what-is-the-water-footprint-of/.

20   Some tasty vegetarian recipe sites are: So Vegan (https://www.wearesovegan.com/), The Chutney Life (https://thechutneylife.com/), and Plant You (https://thechutneylife.com/).

21   "UN Helps Fashion Industry Shift to Low Carbon," United Nations Climate Change, September 6, 2018, https://unfccc.int/news/un-helps-fashion-industry-shift-to-low-carbon.

22   "Carbon Footprint of Tourism," Sustainable Travel International, accessed May 16, 2024, https://sustainabletravel.org/issues/carbon-footprint-tourism/.

23   United States Environmental Protection Agency, "Fast Facts on Transportation Greenhouse Gas Emissions," EPA, October 31, 2023, https://www.epa.gov/greenvehicles/fast-facts-transportation-greenhouse-gas-emissions.

24   Andrew Hawkins "Public Transportation Can Save the World – If We Let it" The Verge, November 1, 2021, https://www.theverge.com/c/22749305/public-transportation-covid-climate-buses-future.

25   Jaime Thilman, "Home Care and Cleaning Routines Go Green," Well+Good, Wellness Trends 2022 – Home, accessed May 21, 2024, https://www.wellandgood.com/2022-fitness-wellness-trends/home/sustainable-cleaning-products/.

26   "Sustainability in Skincare: What Is It?" Comfort Zone Conscious Skin Care, March 1, 2023, https://www.theverge.com/c/22749305/public-transportation-covid-climate-buses-future.

27   https://seadropskincare.com/

28   https://www.sixgldn.com/

29   Jennifer Wu, "ESG outlook 2022: The future of ESG investing," J.P. Morgan Asset Management, https://am.jpmorgan.com/us/en/asset-management/institutional/investment-strategies/sustainable-investing/future-of-esg-investing/.

30   Hanna Ritchie, "Food waste is responsible for 6% of global greenhouse gas emissions," Our World in Data, March 18, 2020, https://ourworldindata.org/food-waste-emissions.

31   "Facts & Figures," Our Last Straw, 2023, https://www.ourlaststraw.org/facts-figures.

32   Tyler Bethke, "PromoLeaf's Green Jobs Report 2022," Green Job Reports, June 9, 2022, https://promoleaf.com/blog/green-job-reports.

33   Emma Ross, "Fast Fashion Getting Faster: A Look at the Unethical Labor Practices Sustaining a Growing Industry," GW Law, October 28, 2021, https://studentbriefs.law.gwu.edu/ilpb/2021/10/28/fast-fashion-getting-faster-a-look-at-the-unethical-labor-practices-sustaining-a-growing-industry/.

34   Lauren Murphy, "Skip the Plastic Wrap: 4 Food Wrap Alternatives," Earth 911, August 17, 2020, https://earth911.com/home-garden/4-food-wrap-alternatives/.

35   EarthDay.org, "A Billion Acts of Green: Slaying Vampire Energy," EarthDay.org, August 15, 2013, https://www.earthday.org/a-billion-acts-of-green-slaying-vampire-energy/#:~:text=100%20billion%20kilowatt%20hours%20of,our%20wallets%20and%20our%20environment.

36   World Wild Fund for Nature, "Living Planet Report 2022," WWF, 2022, https://livingplanet.panda.org/en-US/.

37   Hanna Ritchie, "Dairy vs. plant-based milk: what are the environmental impacts?" Our World in Data, January 19, 2022, https://ourworldindata.org/environmental-impact-milks.

38   https://us.oatly.com/products/oatmilk

39   April Day, "World Water Demand Will Increase 55% by 2050," Save The Water, September 20, 2019, https://savethewater.org/water-demand-to-increase-55-globally-by-2050/.

- -

40   Kip Andersen, Keegan Kuhn, "Cowspiracy: The Sustainability Secret," Netflix, video, 1:30:00, accessed February 14, 2024, https://www.netflix.com/ca/title/80033772

Matt D'Avella,"The Minimalists: Less is Now," Netflix, video, 53:00, accessed February 14, 2024, https://www.netflix.com/ca/title/81074662.

Woody Harrelson, "Kiss the Ground," Netflix, video, 1:24:00, accessed February 14, 2024, https://www.netflix.com/ca/title/81321999.

Lesley Chilcott, "A Small Section of the World," video, 1:02:00, accessed February 14, 2024, https://www.justwatch.com/us/movie/a-small-section-of-the-world.

Joe Caterini, Lydia Tenaglia, "Wasted! The Story of Food Waste," Prime Video, video, 1:25:00, accessed February 14, 2024, https://www.amazon.com/gp/video/detail/0OBAC6TPX93M83BSCTMD1HW70N/ref=atv_dl_rdr?tag=justuscock-20.

Josh Tickell, Kiss the Ground: How the Food You Eat Can Reverse Climate Change, Heal Your Body & Ultimately Save Our World (Dover, USA: Enliven, 2016).

- -

41   greenorb, "88 New Sustainable Statistics and Facts that will Shock You," Thinking Sustainably, May 24, 2022, https://www.thinkingsustainably.com/88-sustainable-statistics/.

- -

42   David Lin, Mathis Wackernagel, and Leopold Wambersie, "Estimating the Date of Earth Overshoot Day 2023," Global Footprint Network, May 2023, https://www.overshootday.org/content/uploads/2023/06/Earth-Overshoot-Day-2023-Nowcast-Report.pdf.

- -

43   https://www.browngirlgreen.com, https://www.savetheplanetpodcast.com

- -

44   Abigail Beall, "Why clothes are so hard to recycle," BBC, July 12, 2020, https://www.bbc.com/future/article/20200710-why-clothes-are-so-hard-to-recycle.

- -

45   Denise Baden, "How to reduce the carbon footprint from your hair care and cosmetics," Ethical Consumer, December 8, 2023, https://www.ethicalconsumer.org/health-beauty/how-reduce-carbon-footprint-your-hair-care.

- -

46   Lorenzo Tondo, "Sea urchin in Sicily at risk of extinction due to popularity as culinary delicacy," The Guardian, November 27, 2023, https://www.theguardian.com/environment/2023/nov/27/sea-urchin-in-sicily-at-risk-of-extinction.

- -

47   Tadashi, "Overfishing Facts," Facts.com, December 30. 2023, https://facts.net/overfishing-facts/.

48   Celia Topping, "Dishwasher vs hand washing: which is greener?" Ovo Energy, May 4, 2021, https://www.ovoenergy.com/guides/energy-guides/dishwasher-vs-hand-washing.

49   "10 Shocking Facts About Waste to Inspire You to Live More Sustainably," Eco Friendly Habits, https://www.ecofriendlyhabits.com/facts-about-waste/.

50   U.S. Department of Energy, "LED Lighting," Energy.gov, January 26, 2024, https://www.energy.gov/energysaver/led-lighting.

51   "Your Trees Matter. Here's How 1 Tree Impacts Our World," The Environmentor, January 26, 2024, https://blog.tentree.com/your-trees-matter-heres-how-1-tree-impacts-our-world/.

52   Tiffany Ayuda, "Your Guide to Buying and Drinking Truly Sustainable Wine," Well+Good, March 5, 2020, https://www.wellandgood.com/what-is-sustainable-wine/.

"What is Sustainable Wine & What Does It Mean for Me?" Bright Cellars, April 22, 2021, https://www.brightcellars.com/blogs/learn/what-is-sustainable-wine-what-does-it-mean-for-me.

53   "Carbon Footprint of Tourism," Sustainable Travel International, accessed May 16, 2024, https://sustainabletravel.org/issues/carbon-footprint-tourism/.

54   Branka Vuleta, "Plastic Waste Statistics: A Deep-Dive," Seed Scientific, March 31, 2022, https://seedscientific.com/environment/plastic-waste-statistics/#:~:text=Single-use%20plastic%20waste%20statistics%20show%20380%20million%20tons,kitchen%20utensils%20are%20used%20and%20discarded%20each%20year.

55   "What Are the Environmental Benefits of Solar Energy?" Solar Melon, 2017, https://www.solarmelon.com/blog/environmental-benefits-solar-energy/.

56   Emily Brock, "ESG on the Ballot: U.S. Proxy Season Preview," ERM Sustainability Institute, February 15, 2023, https://www.sustainability.com/thinking/esg-on-the-ballot-u.s.-proxy-season-preview/.

57   "4 ways to use less paper at home," UNICEF Armenia, June 5, 2020, https://www.unicef.org/armenia/en/stories/4-ways-use-less-paper-home.

58   Sophie Boehm and Clea Schumer, "10 Big Findings from the 2023 IPCC Report on Climate Change," World Resource Institute, March 20, 2023, https://www.wri.org/insights/2023-ipcc-ar6-synthesis-report-climate-change-findings.

www.ingramcontent.com/pod-product-compliance
Lightning Source LLC
Chambersburg PA
CBHW061226270326
41928CB00024B/3345